PUERTO RICO

The All-Star Island

BY
JOHN HAMILTON

Abdo & Daughters

An imprint of Abdo Publishing | abdopublishing.com

abdopublishing.com

Published by ABDO Publishing, a division of ABDO, PO Box 398166, Minneapolis, Minnesota 55439. Copyright © 2017 by Abdo Consulting Group, Inc. International copyrights reserved in all countries. No part of this book may be reproduced in any form without written permission from the publisher. ABDO & Daughters™ is a trademark and logo of ABDO Publishing.

Printed in the United States of America, North Mankato, Minnesota.
062016
092016

THIS BOOK CONTAINS
RECYCLED MATERIALS

Editor: Sue Hamilton   **Contributing Editor:** Bridget O'Brien
Graphic Design: Sue Hamilton
Cover Art Direction: Candice Keimig   **Cover Photo Selection:** Neil Klinepier
Cover Photo: iStock
Interior Images: Alamy, AP, Brendon M, Dreamstime, Getty, iStock, Lev Frid, Library of Congress, Mile High Maps, Mountain High Maps, One Mile Up, Puerto Rico Tsunami Warning and Mitigation Program, RavenFire Media, Roosevelt Roads Naval Base, and Wikimedia.

Statistics: *State and City Populations*, U.S. Census Bureau, July 1, 2015 estimates; *Land and Water Area*, U.S. Census Bureau, 2010 Census, MAF/TIGER database; *State Temperature Extremes*, NOAA National Climatic Data Center; *Climatology and Average Annual Precipitation*, NOAA National Climatic Data Center, 1980-2015 statewide averages; *State Highest and Lowest Points*, NOAA National Geodetic Survey.

Websites: To learn more about the United States, visit booklinks.abdopublishing.com. These links are routinely monitored and updated to provide the most current information available.

Cataloging-in-Publication Data

Names: Hamilton, John, 1959- author.
Title: Puerto Rico / by John Hamilton.
Description: Minneapolis, MN : Abdo Publishing, [2017] | Series: The United
    States of America | Includes index.
Identifiers: LCCN 2015957738 | ISBN 9781680783414 (lib. bdg.) |
    ISBN 9781680774450 (ebook)
Subjects: LCSH: Puerto Rico--Juvenile literature.
Classification: DDC 972.95--dc23
LC record available at http://lccn.loc.gov/2015957738

CONTENTS

THE ALL-STAR ISLAND

Puerto Rico is often called "The Island of Enchantment." It is like a green jewel in the Caribbean Sea. Just 111 miles (179 km) long and 39 miles (63 km) wide, it is filled with sandy beaches, lush rain forests, palm trees, and tropical breezes. But it is Puerto Rico's 3.5 million Spanish- and English-speaking people that make the island truly magical.

A mix of European, African, and native heritage, Puerto Ricans embrace a culture that dates back more than 500 years. In the capital of San Juan, cobblestone streets and massive Spanish forts exist alongside gleaming office towers, nightclubs, and modern art districts.

The island's official name is the "Commonwealth of Puerto Rico." It is a self-governing part of the United States, but it is not a state. Puerto Rico is filled with talented people, and has great business potential. That is why its official slogan is "The All-Star Island."

People walk across the cobblestone streets of Old San Juan. Visitors enjoy the island's beautiful weather and quaint shops.

A lookout point at Castillo San Felipe del Morro in San Juan, Puerto Rico.

QUICK FACTS

Name: Puerto Rico is a Spanish phrase that means "rich port."

Capital: San Juan, population 355,074

Date of Commonwealth: July 25, 1952

Population: 3,474,182

Area (Total Land and Water): 5,325 square miles (13,792 sq km)

Largest City: San Juan, population 355,074

Nicknames: All-Star Island; Island of Enchantment

Motto: *Joannes Est Nomen Eius* (John is his name)

National Bird: Reina Mora (Puerto Rican Spindalis)

National Flower: Puerto Rican Hibiscus

National Tree: Kapok (*Ceiba pentandra*)

National Anthem: "La Borinqueña"

Highest Point: Cerro de Punta, 4,390 feet (1,338 m)

Lowest Point: Caribbean Sea, 0 feet (0 m)

Cerro de Punta

Average July High Temperature (San Juan): 89°F (32°C)

Record High Temperature: 104°F (40°C), on Mona Island on July 2, 1996

Average January Low Temperature (San Juan): 71°F (22°C)

Record Low Temperature: 40°F (4°C), in Rincon on March 27, 1985

Caribbean Sea

SAN JUAN, PUERTO RICO
U.S. 8¢
1521-1971

Average Annual Precipitation (San Juan): 57 inches (145 cm)

Number of U.S. Senators: 0

Number of U.S. Representatives: 0

U.S. Postal Service Abbreviation: PR

GEOGRAPHY

Puerto Rico is a group of islands in the Caribbean Sea. It is part of a chain of large islands called the Greater Antilles. They are part of a larger region of islands called the West Indies.

West of Puerto Rico is the island of Hispaniola, which includes the countries of Haiti and the Dominican Republic. The two islands are separated by a body of water called the Mona Passage. East of Puerto Rico are the Virgin Islands. To the north is the Atlantic Ocean, and to the south is the Caribbean Sea.

Puerto Rico is about 1,000 miles (1,609 km) southeast of Florida. It is an archipelago, made up of several islands. Puerto Rico is the name of the biggest island in the group. There are several smaller islands, including Culebra, Mona, Desecheo, Caja de Muertos, and Vieques.

Culebra Island

The island of Puerto Rico is in the Caribbean
Sea. Puerto Rico's total land and water area
is 5,325 square miles (13,792 sq km). The
capital and largest city is San Juan.

The main island of Puerto Rico is shaped roughly like a rectangle. It measures approximately 111 miles (179 km) long and 39 miles (63 km) wide. Its land area covers 3,424 square miles (8,868 sq km).

Along the northern and southern coasts are narrow strips of land called the Coastal Lowlands. Puerto Rico's largest cities, including the capital of San Juan, are located in the Coastal Lowlands. There are also farms that grow fruits and vegetables, or raise poultry and dairy cows.

Most of Puerto Rico is hilly or mountainous. The largest mountain range is the Cordillera Central, or Central Mountains. It runs east and west across the middle of the island. The highest point in Puerto Rico is in these mountains. It is Cerro de Punta, which soars 4,390 feet (1,338 m) above sea level. In the cool, moist mountain regions are many coffee plantations.

Cueva Ventana, or Window Cave, is in the northwestern region of Puerto Rico.

In the northwest, between the Central Mountains and the Coastal Lowlands, is a large region called the Puerto Rican karst. It is made of eroded limestone and dolomite. There are many caves, sinkholes, and underground rivers in the karst.

Because of the mountains that run east and west, and because the island is so short in width, there are few long rivers in Puerto Rico. The longest rivers include the Loísa, Arecibo, and La Plata Rivers. There are hundreds of smaller mountain streams. Puerto Rico has 15 man-made reservoirs created by damming the rivers. They provide some electricity and water for irrigation.

GEOGRAPHY

CLIMATE AND
WEATHER

Puerto Rico has a warm, tropical climate. Temperatures stay about the same throughout the year. There are many sunny, breezy days. The average temperature is about 80°F (27°C). Temperatures are cooler in the high mountains in the central part of the island.

Warm winds that blow in from the ocean carry a lot of water vapor. When clouds rise over the high mountains, the water vapor cools. It condenses and falls to the ground as rain. Some of Puerto Rico's mountain areas receive more than 200 inches (508 cm) of rain yearly. Rainfall varies all across the island. Along the northern coast, in the city of San Juan, average yearly rainfall is 57 inches (145 cm).

Hurricane Georges struck Puerto Rico in 1998. The violent hurricane crossed the entire island and caused eight deaths and $2 billion in damage.

Puerto Rico is sometimes struck by violent hurricanes that blow in from the Atlantic Ocean. When Hurricane Georges struck in 1998, it killed eight people and caused more than $2 billion in damage. The hurricane season lasts from about June through November.

PLANTS AND
ANIMALS

**El Yunque
National Forest**

Puerto Rico is rich in plants and vegetation. On the north side of the island, where there is the most rain, there are tropical rain forests. They are filled with more than 500 kinds of trees, plus brightly colored plants and flowers.

El Yunque National Forest is on the northeastern side of the island. It is the only rain forest in the national forest system. It protects 29,000 acres (11,736 ha) of land. Tucked within the steep slopes of the Luquillo Mountains, there are hundreds of plants and animals found nowhere else on Earth. The forest is home to 150 species of ferns, 240 species of trees, and wildflowers such as orchids.

Poinciana, or Flame Tree

Kapok (center) is the national tree of Puerto Rico.

Dense forests once covered almost all of Puerto Rico. Most of the trees were cut down by the early 1900s. In the 1930s, the Puerto Rican government began a program to replant trees. Today, many kinds of plants thrive on the island. They include poinciana, kapok, bougainvillea, sierra and coconut palm, breadfruit, and tree ferns. Cactus and bunch grass grow in the southwestern part of the island, where there is less rain.

PLANTS AND ANIMALS

No large, wild mammals are found on Puerto Rico. Several species of bats are native to the island. During colonial days, Spanish settlers imported pigs, horses, and cows. In the 1800s, small Asian mongooses were brought to the island by farmers. They wanted the mongooses to help control the many rats that had infested Puerto Rico's sugarcane fields. The experiment failed, however. The mongooses preferred to eat Puerto Rico's many bird species. Today, mongooses are found over much of the island.

Despite the mongoose invasion, there are more than 200 species of birds living on the island. They include the bright-green Puerto Rican parrot. Endangered brown pelicans are found on the island of Culebra. Other seabirds include gulls, terns, and frigate birds. The reina mora is the national bird. Also called the Puerto Rican spindalis, males of the species are brightly colored, with a black-and-white face pattern and an orange-brown chest.

Puerto Rican parrots are the only parrot species native to the islands. They almost died out in the 1970s. Although still endangered, their numbers have increased.

Coquí

There are dozens of species of reptiles and amphibians in Puerto Rico. The coquí is a small tree frog found only in Puerto Rico. It has a loud croak that sounds like its name: "co-kee." Large iguanas can sometimes be spotted basking along the seashore. There are 11 species of snakes on the island, all considered non-venomous. The Puerto Rican boa can grow up to 12 feet (3.7 m) in length.

Fish and other sea creatures living in the waters around Puerto Rico include kingfish, barracuda, tuna, mullet, mackerel, dolphin, lobster, and oysters.

Iguana

HISTORY

Taíno Man

People have lived on the island of Puerto Rico for more than 4,000 years. Historians don't know much about the earliest inhabitants. Over the centuries, various tribes came by boat to live on the island. They included the Igneri people. They hunted and fished, and lived in small villages along the coast.

About 1100 AD, the Taíno people arrived. They settled on many Caribbean islands, including Puerto Rico. The Taíno lived in wooden huts in large villages. They hunted, fished, and grew crops such as yams and beans. They were also woodworkers, and made gold and shell jewelry.

Christopher Columbus visited Puerto Rico on his second voyage in 1493.

In 1493, Italian explorer Christopher Columbus set foot on Puerto Rico during his second voyage to the New World. Since he was working for the monarchs of Spain, he declared that the island was Spanish property, even though thousands of Taíno people were already living there.

Columbus named the island "San Juan Bautista," in honor of the Christian saint, John the Baptist. Years later, the island's largest city also became known as San Juan. The city had a bustling seaport. The Spanish phrase *puerto rico* means "rich port." Over time, the entire island became known as Puerto Rico.

Conquistador Juan Ponce de León explored the island of Puerto Rico in 1508. He looked for gold and searched for places to start Spanish settlements.

In 1508, Juan Ponce de León from Spain arrived in Puerto Rico. He started the first European settlement on the island, called Caparra. The following year, he declared himself governor. As the Spanish began to colonize Puerto Rico, large numbers of the native Taíno people died. Thousands succumbed to diseases such as smallpox and measles, which were brought accidentally to the island by the Spaniards. Other natives were killed by warfare, or forced into slavery. The Spanish began shipping thousands of African slaves to Puerto Rico to work on large farms called plantations.

Life in Puerto Rico was difficult throughout the 1500s, 1600s, and 1700s. Pirates continually harassed the settlers. Soldiers from competing countries, including the English, French, and Dutch, often raided the island's cities. Native tribes from neighboring islands attacked farms and small towns.

To protect themselves from raids, the Spanish built huge forts made of stone. In the 1500s, they built Castillo San Felipe del Morro at the entrance to the Port of San Juan. Some of the fort's outer stone walls are 18 feet (5 m) thick. In the 1700s, the Spanish built an even bigger fort called Castillo San Cristóbal. Many of these forts still stand today, and are popular tourist attractions.

By the 1830s, business on Puerto Rico thrived. Huge plantations grew profitable crops such as sugarcane and coffee. Much of the work on the plantations was done by African slaves.

An aerial view of Castillo San Felipe del Morro, which was built in the 1500s.

In 1898, American warships fired at Spanish ships and on Castillo San Felipe del Morro at San Juan, Puerto Rico.

In 1898, the United States fought the Spanish-American War. With its superior military, the United States won the war in less than four months. As part of the peace agreement, Spain gave up several of its island colonies, including Puerto Rico. The United States set up a government on the island.

By 1917, the people of Puerto Rico became United States citizens. In the 1930s, there were calls for Puerto Rican independence. Some protests were violent, but Puerto Rico remained dependent on the United States.

During World War II (1939-1945), the United States Navy built a large naval air station in San Juan. During the war, more than 65,000 Puerto Ricans served in the Unites States armed forces.

After the war, hundreds of manufacturing plants were built on the island. Companies received big tax breaks from the government, which made moving to Puerto Rico more profitable.

In the 1950s, Puerto Rico gained more control over its affairs. In 1952, the island became a commonwealth of the United States. The Puerto Rican government can make its own laws and elect its own governor. People of the island remain United States citizens, but they may not vote in presidential elections.

In recent years, Puerto Rico has suffered from much government debt that it has struggled to repay. Services have been cut, and people have lost jobs. Many have migrated to the U.S. mainland. Big companies remain, however, and the island has become a major tourist destination, boosting the local economy.

On July 22, 1952, a parade celebrated Puerto Rico's new constitution, which established the island as a commonwealth.

DID YOU KNOW?

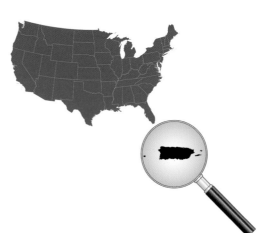

• Arecibo Observatory is one of the largest radio telescopes on Earth. Located in northwestern Puerto Rico, its curved dish measures 1,000 feet (305 m) across. It was built inside a large sinkhole. It uses radio waves to observe distant objects in our solar system such as planets and asteroids. It also searches for radio signals that might have been sent by civilizations on alien worlds.

• Deadly earthquakes sometimes strike Puerto Rico. In 1918, a magnitude 7.5 earthquake occurred on the ocean floor near the island's northwestern coast. The shaking caused buildings and bridges to collapse. It also caused a terrifying tsunami that swamped the northern and western shores of the island. The quake and tsunami killed 116 people and caused millions of dollars in damage.

• Today, Puerto Rico is a commonwealth. The United States has sovereignty, which means it rules the island, even though Puerto Ricans pass their own laws and elect their own local leaders. Many residents want the island to become the 51st state of the United States. They say it will be easier to bring new businesses to the island. The U.S. government, they hope, would also help build bridges, roads, and schools. Being a state would also mean Puerto Rico would have representatives in Congress, and citizens could vote in presidential elections.

Many other Puerto Ricans want the island to remain a commonwealth. They fear a higher cost of living, and a loss of Puerto Rican culture. A smaller minority of citizens prefer total independence in order to start a new country. It is a question that will have to eventually be decided by the United States Congress and the people of Puerto Rico.

DID YOU KNOW?

PEOPLE

Roberto Clemente (1934-1972) was one of the greatest professional baseball players of all time. He was born in the Puerto Rican city of Carolina. As a boy, when he wasn't working alongside his father in the sugarcane fields, he learned to play baseball. He became a pro player at age 18. He became so good that in 1954, the Pittsburgh Pirates offered him a Major League Baseball contract. He played right field for 18 years for the Pirates. He won the Gold Glove Award 12 times. In 1966, he was the National League's Most Valuable Player. He had 3,000 hits during his career. In 1972, he was traveling to Nicaragua to help earthquake victims when his plane crashed, killing him. Clemente was posthumously inducted into the Baseball Hall of Fame in 1973.

Agüeybaná (?-1510) was one of the most powerful chiefs of the Taíno people in the late 1400s and early 1500s. When Christopher Columbus and other Spaniards first arrived in Puerto Rico in 1493, Agüeybaná was there to greet them. He also met Juan Ponce de León when the Spanish conquistador arrived in 1508. Agüeybaná wanted friendly relations with the Spanish settlers. He helped them explore the island. Tragically, the Taíno people's hospitality was betrayed by the Spaniards, who eventually conquered the island and enslaved many of the natives. When Agüeybaná died in 1510, his brother led a revolt against the invaders. The natives faced the Spaniard's superior weapons, including guns, and were easily defeated. Many natives later died because of diseases brought to the island by the Spanish conquerors.

Ricky Martin (1971-) is a Grammy Award-winning pop singer who has sold tens of millions of records worldwide. He was born Enrique Martín Morales in San Juan, Puerto Rico. At age 13, he began singing with the popular boy band Menudo. After five years with the band, he released a string of Spanish-language solo pop albums. In 1999, he won a Grammy Award for Best Latin Pop Album for *Vuelve*. He released his first self-titled English-language album in 1999. The first hit from the album was the number-one smash "Livin' la Vida Loca" (Spanish for "the crazy life"). Martin is famous for his electrifying live stage performances. He continues to record hit music. He won his second Best Latin Pop Album Grammy Award in 2016 for *A Quien Quiera Escuchar* (To Those Who Want to Listen).

Sila María Calderón (1942-) is a successful Puerto Rican businesswoman and politician. She served as the eighth governor of the commonwealth from 2001 to 2005. As the island's first elected woman governor, she combated poverty by trying to create jobs and eliminate corruption in government. Before becoming governor, she was elected mayor of San Juan, serving from 1997 to 2001. Calderón was born in San Juan.

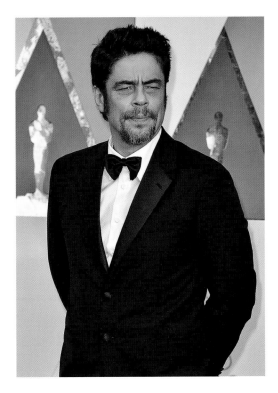

Benicio del Toro (1967-) is an Academy Award-winning Hollywood actor. After a string of television and movie appearances in the 1980s, his breakout role came in 1995 as Fred Fenster in *The Usual Suspects*. He won an Academy Award for his performance in 2000's *Traffic*. He has starred in many movies since, including *The Wolfman*, *Guardians of the Galaxy*, and *Sicario*. Del Toro was born in San Juan.

CITIES

San Juan is the biggest city in Puerto Rico. It is also the commonwealth's capital. Its population is about 355,074. It is located on the northeastern coast of the island. The city was founded in 1508 by Spanish conquistador Juan Ponce de León. It is one of the oldest cities in the Western Hemisphere. The Spanish began building massive stone forts starting in the 1530s to protect San Juan from pirates and other hostile nations. Today, the forts and hundreds of other historic buildings are popular tourist attractions. Visitors also enjoy San Juan's many museums, art galleries, shops, and sandy beaches. The city is a center for banking and manufacturing. There are several colleges in San Juan, including the main campus of the University of Puerto Rico.

The city of **Bayamón** is just to the southwest of San Juan. It is Puerto Rico's second-most populous city, with a population of about 189,159. The city was founded in 1772, and may have taken its name from the Taíno native name of a nearby river. Today, Bayamón has factories that produce goods such as automobile parts and furniture. The city lies in a fertile valley. Surrounding farms produce many kinds of fruits and vegetables, as well as tobacco and coffee. The city is home to Bayamón Central University. The Luis A. Ferré Science Park includes museums, a zoo, and an exhibit of NASA rockets.

Carolina is east of the capital city of San Juan. It is part of the large metropolitan area that includes San Juan, Bayamón, Guaynabo, and Toa Baja. Carolina was founded in 1857. It is often nicknamed *"La Tierra de Gigantes"* (Land of the Giants), in honor of one of its most famous citizens, Felipe Birriel. He was the tallest man in Puerto Rican history, measuring 7' 11" (242 cm) tall. Baseball superstar Roberto Clemente was also born in Carolina. There are many manufacturing companies in Carolina. They produce chemicals, medicines, medical equipment, and other goods. Carolina is a major tourist destination, with many hotels and sandy beaches. Carolina's population is about 161,884.

Felipe Birriel

Ponce is located on the southern coast of Puerto Rico. It is the biggest city outside of the San Juan metropolitan area. Its population is about 149,028. Its nickname is *"La Perla del Sur"* (Pearl of the South). Founded in 1692, it was named after the great-grandson of Spanish conquistador Ponce de León. There are many historic Spanish buildings that are preserved in the city. There are also modern manufacturing centers. Its port is one of the busiest in the Caribbean region. The Ponce Museum of Art showcases more than 1,000 paintings and 400 sculptures, including many by Puerto Rican artists. The Museum of Puerto Rican Music traces the island's rich musical heritage, including displays of Spanish, African, and native instruments.

TRANSPORTATION

Puerto Rico has 16,691 miles (26,862 km) of public roadways. A highway system circles the main island along the coast. Several roads also cross the mountains, linking the north side of Puerto Rico with the south.

In the late 1800s and early 1900s, a large system of railroads was built across the island. Railroads were mainly used to haul crops, especially sugarcane. Today, the railroads have been almost completely replaced by cars and trucks.

Puerto Rico has a coastal highway system that circles the main island.

Luis Muñoz Marín International Airport handles almost nine million passengers yearly.

Luis Muñoz Marín International Airport is in the city of Carolina, just east of the capital city of San Juan. It is one of the busiest airports in the Caribbean region, handling almost nine million passengers yearly. There are also large airports in Aguadilla, Ponce, and Ceiba.

Puerto Rico has three major ports. The Port of San Juan is the busiest. Much of the island's imported food and other goods come through this port. Many cruise ships also use the Port of San Juan. The Port of Ponce, on the south side of the island, also handles cargo and cruise ships. The Port of Mayagüez, on the western coast, handles mostly freight.

TRANSPORTATION

NATURAL
RESOURCES

Puerto Rico's soil is thin, and large-scale farming is not very profitable. The island imports most of its food. In recent years, the government has tried to encourage more locally grown crops.

Farming was once a big part of life on the island. Sugarcane was especially important. In the 1900s, the government encouraged people to work in factories instead of on farms. The large sugarcane fields went out of business.

A coffee farm in Maricao, Puerto Rico.

Today, farming only accounts for less than one percent of the commonwealth's economy. There are about 13,000 farms on the island. Most are very small, and their crops are sold locally. Top crops include coffee, plantains, oranges, and a variety of other fruits and vegetables. Livestock includes poultry, hogs, rabbits, and sheep. Dairy farming is a very profitable business for some farmers.

Puerto Rico's mining industry is small. The most profitable items dug from the Earth include lime, crushed stone, plus sand and gravel. There are deposits of copper, gold, silver, and zinc on the island, but they are not mined on a large scale.

INDUSTRY

Since the 1940s, the government has worked hard to attract new factories to Puerto Rico. Today, manufacturing accounts for more than 45 percent of the commonwealth's economy. The majority of the island's factories are centered around the San Juan metropolitan area. Puerto Rico is a big producer of medicines, chemicals, food products, electronic equipment, and clothing.

The finance, real estate, and insurance industries make up about 20 percent of Puerto Rico's economy. The island uses the United States dollar as its currency. Its most important trading partner by far is the United States, although its does business with other countries such as Japan, the Dominican Republic, and some European nations. Its main exports are medicines, chemicals, and machinery.

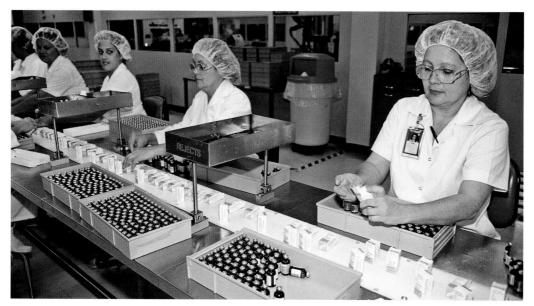

Workers package bottles at a pharmaceutical factory in Puerto Rico.

Tourists enjoy Isla Verde Beach in Carolina, Puerto Rico.

Today, tourism is a very important part of Puerto Rico's economy. More than four million people visit each year, attracted to the island's historic sites, year-round warm weather, sandy beaches, museums, and shopping. The tourism industry supports about 70,000 jobs on the island.

SPORTS

The most popular sport in Puerto Rico, by far, is baseball. Many people play in island leagues and clubs. Hundreds of Puerto Rican baseball players have gone on to careers in Major League Baseball in the United States mainland.

The Puerto Rico National Baseball Team represents the island in international competitions. It has won many championship medals in events such as the Baseball World Cup and the World Baseball Classic.

Other popular sports in the commonwealth include soccer, boxing, golf, and basketball. There are many amateur clubs and professional franchises that compete all over the island.

Puerto Rican teammates celebrate a home run during a World Baseball Classic game. Baseball is the most popular sport in Puerto Rico.

Puerto Rico's Javier Culson won a bronze medal in the men's 400-meter hurdles during the 2012 Summer Olympic Games in London, England.

Since 1948, Puerto Rico has competed in the Summer and Winter Olympic Games as an independent nation. As American citizens, Puerto Ricans have the option of moving to the United States mainland for three years in order to represent the U.S. instead. Puerto Rico has won eight Olympic medals. Six were for boxing, one was for wrestling, and one was for the men's 400-meter hurdles.

Puerto Rico's coasts are ideal for many outdoor sports. The island's sandy beaches are great for swimming, boating, and fishing. Puerto Rico's steady warm temperatures make it a good place for tennis and golf.

ENTERTAINMENT

Traditional Puerto Rican Dancers

The capital city of San Juan is a center for the arts. There are many opera and classical music halls, as well as jazz and rock clubs. Dance troupes are very common. Music and dance are treasured by Puerto Rican culture. Musicians and dancers from the island helped develop the styles of Latin jazz and salsa. Many popular songs and dances are based on Spanish and African folk songs.

For hundreds of years, Puerto Rico was a colony of Spain. Many of the commonwealth's buildings still have Spanish architecture. The oldest part of San Juan contains huge fortresses built by the Spanish military to defend against pirates and hostile nations. Castillo San Felipe del Morro guards the entrance to the Port of San Juan. Built in the 1500s, some of the fort's outer stone walls are 18 feet (5 m) thick. It survived several attacks over the years. Today, it is a popular tourist attraction. More than 2 million people explore the stone fortress each year.

Camuy River Cave is the third-largest underground cave system in the world. Inside the natural wonder are stalagmites and stalactites, thousands of bats, and the sounds of the Río Camuy, an underground river that created the cave.

At the Camuy River Cave Park, in the northwestern part of the island, visitors can easily explore fern-filled limestone caves and sinkholes. Water carved these cathedral-like caverns more than one million years ago. There are many walking trails.

TIMELINE

2000 BC—The first inhabitants of Puerto Rico arrive on the island.

1100 AD—The Taíno people arrive from South America.

1493—Columbus lands on Puerto Rico.

1508-1509—Juan Ponce de León, a Spanish conquistador, invades Puerto Rico and becomes the island's governor.

1500s—The fortress of San Felipe del Morro is built to protect the Port of San Juan.

1898—Spain and the United States fight the Spanish-American War. The victorious United States gains control of Puerto Rico.

1917—Puerto Ricans become United States citizens.

1918—A powerful earthquake and tsunami kill 116 people and cause millions of dollars in damage.

1941-1945—The United States builds an important naval base in San Juan during World War II.

1952—Puerto Ricans vote to become a commonwealth of the United States.

1955—Roberto Clemente of Puerto Rico joins Major League Baseball's Pittsburgh Pirates.

2003—Because of protests, the United States Navy stops airplane bombing training on Vieques, a small island east of the main island of Puerto Rico.

2012—During the London Summer Olympic Games, Jaime Espinal wins a silver medal in wrestling and Javier Culson wins a bronze medal in the men's 400-meter hurdles.

2016—Puerto Rico suffers a debt crisis that forces many government services to be suspended.

GLOSSARY

ARCHIPELAGO

A group of islands. Puerto Rico is an archipelago that contains a large main island (named Puerto Rico) and several much smaller islands nearby.

BREADFRUIT

A starchy fruit often cooked or used in place of flour.

CARIBBEAN

An area of the Atlantic Ocean south of Puerto Rico and north of South America.

COMMONWEALTH

A self-governing territory that is voluntarily part of another country. Puerto Rico is a commonwealth of the United States. Although not an official state, Puerto Ricans are citizens of the U.S.

CONQUISTADOR

Spanish soldiers and explorers who came to the Americas in the 1500s. They used force to conquer native people and take control of their lands.

HYDROELECTRIC POWER

When rivers are dammed, a controlled flow of water runs turbines, which drive generators that create electricity.

Plantation

A large farm where crops such as coffee, sugar, or tobacco are raised by people who live on the estate. In Puerto Rico's early history, African slaves were forced to work on large sugarcane and coffee plantations.

Salsa

A kind of Latin American dance music. Salsa is a fusion of jazz and rock. The term also refers to the dance that is performed to salsa music.

Sinkhole

A depression or hole in the ground that is formed when an underground chamber forms, such as a limestone cave, and the top layer collapses into it. There are many sinkholes in northwestern Puerto Rico.

Spanish-American War

A war started in April 1898 between Spain and the United States. The war was fought to help the islands of Puerto Rico, Cuba, and the Philippines gain freedom from Spain. The war ended in August 1898 with Spain giving up the islands.

Tsunami

A large sea wave that is created by earthquakes or underwater landslides. When tsunamis strike land, they can be very destructive.

World War II

A conflict that was fought from 1939 to 1945, involving countries around the world. The United States entered the war after Japan bombed the American naval base at Pearl Harbor, in Oahu, Hawaii, on December 7, 1941.

INDEX